I0475987

SYNERGISTIC CAPITALISM

A New Approach to Economics

by

Stuart "Boot" Gordon, M.Ed.

Copyright © by Gordonstown Press.
All rights reserved. No portion of this
book may be reproduced in any form
without permission from publisher for
commercial purposes.
Gordonstown Press
PO Box 1929, Silverthorne, Colorado 80498

Create Space
ISBN-13: 978-1502525611
ISBN-10: 1502525615

Other Books by Stuart "Boot" Gordon, M. Ed.

Artivity, An Approach To Art Through Six Art Activities

Gordonstown, A New Design for America

Skiing with a Boot

Pre-Skiing Primer

Ski Powder 5 Ways

Light Talk For My Grandkids

Clear It, For God's Sake

About Stuart "Boot" Gordon, M. Ed.

Originator of the Peace Corps, Canoe and Mountain Guide,
Ski Instructor, Salesman, Teacher, Combat Fighter Pilot,
Purchasing and Contracting Officer, Inventor, Designer,
Author, Builder

SYNERGISTIC CAPITALISM
by Stuart "Boot" Gordon, M.Ed.

FOREWORD

I often wear my WWII baseball cap with little pins of airplanes I flew, so people have an opportunity to be nice to me. (Translation: so I get attention.) And often people come up to me and say, "Thank you for your service."

I thank them then add, "Would you please stop all these wars? They're all contrived." Without exception they nod in agreement. Some even add, "Yes, Eisenhower warned us about the military-industrial complex."

Thus I wondered why do we let the "secret government" run our country, our foreign affairs, our armed forces and our economy?

Then I realize they're scared; they have families, car and house payments. And they know they are three pay checks away from starvation. "So Wall Street and those in power are making millions, at least I have a job," they seem to be saying. And they seem to intuitively know that the "powers that be" can easily create a world-wide depression that would collapse our economy (like they did in 1929?)

And what's the alternative

Well, here's another approach to economics which could work, you decide.

A LITTLE BACKGROUND

After my P-51 Minnesota Air National Guard squadron was deactivated after the Korean "War," I returned to college and got a masters degree in education. While studying I designed a program for teenagers called the Trail Corps, a combination private school and the CCC program of the 1930's. Purpose? To give kids a chance to build themselves up physically, vent their desire for independence (and discipline?), and to escape the nest.

I remained in the Air Guard, but because the brass wanted young blood, we old WWII pilots were distributed throughout the Wing. I became acting Executive Officer and Training Officer for the 133rd Maintenance Squadron.

After a few months I thought to myself, We aren't going to win the cold war or any war with these guys. Why not send them overseas to help undeveloped countries move into the 21st Century?

I was really excited about the idea which I called the Peace Corps and told my fellow officers in the Air Guard about it. "Good idea, Boot, but no one in Washington will listen to you." " Hubert Humphrey (our Minnesota Senator in Washington) will listen to me." And I sent him a letter explaining, I thought, my Peace Corps idea.

Humphrey answered my letter, complimented me on "the idea," and suggested I write a Senator from South Dakota who was trying to restart the CCC's. I was crestfallen. In fact I felt as if someone had slugged me below my belt.(It turned out that I had send Humphrey my Trail Corps idea.) But I took Humphrey's advice and sent the Peace Corps idea to the senator in South Dakota saying it was much better than the CCC's, how it would link the undeveloped nations to the U.S., etc.

Note: a senator from South Dakota took credit for giving the Peace Corps idea to Humphrey, who gave it to President Kennedy who gave it to his brother-in-law Sargent Shriver.

Then I thought about the concept and decided it was a lousy idea. Who in the undeveloped countries wanted to take orders or advice from a cocky American kid? Yes, building schools and digging wells was nice but what they really wanted was … to live like Americans. They had all seen pictures of our kitchens, bathrooms, and carports in our magazines and movies; how come they couldn't live like we do?

Note: Someone said it wasn't President Reagan's armament program that broke up the Soviet Union, it was the TV series "Dallas."

So I thought, why not export the "American Way" to all those undeveloped countries? And then I realized our "American Way" wasn't the epitome of progress, our city plans needed tweaking: The "City of the Future" needed a New Style of Architecture based on the curve that could be built quickly (spray foam technology), a City Plan that encouraged a sense of community (houses built in clusters, clusters in villages, villages in towns, and towns grouped around the City Center), a New Transportation System (sans autos), a New

<u>Approach to Education </u>(emphasis on pre-birth to age four, and my Trail Corps idea), all in a park like setting.

When people asked, "Hey, Boot, how ya going to pay for all the civic buildings, the parks, the monorail, the school system, cultural events, etc?" I meditated and channeled this approach to economics, Synergistic Capitalism (I take no credit for any of my good ideas.)

Will it work? Here are 3 "proofs."

1. George Pillsbury told me, "Boot, my son Phillip invited a business consultant from San Francisco Louis Kelso to talk to the Board of Directors of Honeywell (or was it Pillsbury?) He's trying to talk the State of Alaska into joint venturing with private enterprises to develop the natural resources of Alaska, which is exactly your approach." (Alaska did so. If you are a resident of Alaska, you get a dividend from the State every year.)

2. A client of mine (who had the largest law firm west of the Mississippi?) when I taught skiing for Stein Ericksen at Snowmass said, "Boot, your idea isn't new; that's what Tito is doing in Yugoslavia."

3. Mondragon, a workers' coop in Spain uses a similar approach. It is now a billion dollar enterprise.

So here, briefly, is Synergistic Capitalism:

INTRODUCTION:

According to business consultant Louis Kelso only one in a thousand in capitalist America is a capitalist (a person who receives at least 51% of his or her income from capital investments).

If this be true, we need to produce more capitalists. Why? Because capitalists have the time and the money to create more businesses, thus more jobs, thus a more vibrant economy.

We can encourage more people to become capitalists by encouraging entrepreneuring. Entrepreneurs provide more opportunities for investors. Entrepreneurs can create businesses that will hire workers who will be able to buy the goods and services that our country needs. If France is the nation of shopkeepers, America is becoming the nation of shoppers. And shoppers don't build a sound economy. Especially if the products they buy are made in China, Japan, South Korea and Singapore.

Synergistic Capitalism was designed to encourage entrepreneurs and capitalism. I believe this new approach to economics will improve not only the economic well-being of our great nation but help to solve some of our social problems.

I knew that synergy existed (it is defined as the interaction of two or more substances or organisms that increases each other's effectiveness so that the result is greater than the sum of its parts.) The local question was, Why not utilize the synergy of people in a town to encourage entrepreneurs so that all would benefit. Thus Synergistic Capitalism was born back in Minnesota in 1955 (it took me a while to listen).

I believe our Nation's prosperity can no longer depend on those individuals espoused by Ayn Rand who can create on their own (Read *Atlas Shrugged*) or by the super rich who can gather the teams and money to develop ideas. We need to involve all who can contribute to a stronger American economy. We need to get more of those 999 of the 1,000 involved.

Why should we worry about the little guy? First, there's a lot of talent and ideas going to waste that could enrichen America. Second, we need consumers who have money to buy the goods and services. Third, we get "brownie points" for helping others.

MAIN TENETS:

1. Towns can make money instead of spending it. Study Zermatt, Switzerland, Vatican City, Italy.
2. Residents live in Castles (high rises) because individual homes create urban sprawl and loss of "sense of community."
3. All land and real estate is owned by the town.
4. The town is owned by its residents not by Wall Street or the Koch Brothers. (Like a Country Club there can be no speculation.)
5. Our Nation's greatest untapped natural resource is the energy, enthusiasm, talents and the creativity (ideas) of each individual.
6. Entrepreneurs can boost the American economy, but only a few currently succeed. Why?
   a. Not many have profitable ideas.
   b. Their business acumen is limited.
   c. They don't have any clout.
   d. They don't have management skills.
   e. They can't raise capital.
   f. They can't market their product or service.
7. Towns can joint venture with entrepreneurs to increase their rate of success. (NOTE: this is not required. Entrepreneurs can "go it alone" or form

private corporations without town participation.)

a. Towns can purchase ideas. (The discovery curve is moving upward exponentially; lots of ideas are available.)

b. The town can provide business advice, research, and rent office or production space at a discount until a start-up company becomes profitable. (Hey, the average Joe can't even balance his own check book.)

c. Towns can provide clout. They're as powerful as state governments especially if they don't take handouts from the Federal Government.

d. The average guy can't manage his own kids, how is he going to manage a work force? So the town provides management (when needed).

e. The average guy can't borrow money at a reasonable rate to repair his home, how is he going to find capital to start a business. (Under capitalization is one of the major causes of bankruptcy.) But towns can raise capital via municipal bonds or from a joint ventured town bank.

f. And the average guy can't talk his girlfriend into hitting the sack when he wants; how, then, can he sell people on his idea or market his product or service? But a town can joint venture with talented marketers to form a marketing company which can market town products and services.

8. Towns can form a Venture Capital Company to create profitable businesses. Most venture capitalists want to fund a start-up like Microsoft and make a killing. So they don't invest in possible profitable but not hugely successful bets.   Private Equity Companies often buy up companies, sell their assets, destroy the company, lay off the workers (a la Mitt Romney's Bain Corporation) and pocket the profits,

Instead, a town can joint venture with an entrepreneur or group of entrepreneurs. The town sees that the business plan is profitable and funds that operation. Unlike usual venture capitalists, the town is interested in not losing money. If the new venture produces a one dollar profit, that's fine because it has provided work for many, and produced wealth that is enjoyed by merchants and others in the town. By the way, Mondragon only had three small business failures and not one investor lost any money. (See Mondragon, TAB A)

9. There's more money to be make in people than in real estate. (And how many real estate offices are there in America?)

10. Towns can profit by taking a percentage of the gross income of each product or service that it helps. The percentage, of course, depends on the value of the town's participation. This then is given to the residents of the town as dividends just like the state of Alaska. (An idea proposed by Louis Kelso.)

11. Management overhead is reduced by salary caps. Mondragon started out with a ratio of 3 to 1 but eventually ended up 7 to 1. In other words the CEO made only seven times the salary of the cleaning lady. I guess the rational was, if you think you're talented and deserve a higher salary, become an entrepreneur and start your own company. Oh yes, there will be no "golden parachutes.

12. Towns can create a bank that is not affiliated with any national bank. It can study the original banks of Iceland, Sweden and North Dakota before the former two consolidated and lost money. And it can study the Mondragon Bank.

DISCUSSION:

You might ask, If the town raises capital via municipal bonds, won't this eliminate the need for investors who want to invest their capital? Won't it reduce opportunities for people to invest? Remember that Louis Kelso, who was a successful business consultant in California, defined a capitalist as a person who made 51% of his income from his capital, i.e. interest from bonds or savings, or stock dividends. Therefore, Kelso claimed that only one in a thousand in America is a capitalist. If we increase the number of capitalists, i.e. members of the town, these capitalists will have more money available to invest, more people will be employed with more money to spend or invest.

NOTE: The town will not own 100% of many if any corporations so there'll be plenty of opportunity to invest.

And Synergistic Capitalism doesn't insist that all entrepreneurs joint venture with the town. Synergistic Capitalism encourages entrepreneurs, all entrepreneurs. If a resident or group of residents have all the talents, capital, etc. needed to start a business, they won't need the town; but the town can offer to critique their business plan for a small fee (no free lunch) or offer business space at low rent for the start-up.

Synergistic Capitalism is, therefore, a pump priming system and educational tool without a Washington bureaucracy or Wall Street leeches.

Synergistic Capitalism can revitalize our political system. At the present time approximately 1 in 1,000 votes in a local election. By combining the social and the political with a community's economic system, perhaps more residents will be concerned about the actions of their local officials. If the taxpayer is renting a small apartment, works in an adjoining town, and owns no land, what does he care how the town's money is spent. But if he owns a share in the town, then he might be quite interested in how HIS money is spent. Townspeople can vote out the bums who can't make money for the town. Residents will vote in those who can. Such a system can be quite efficient because the decisions and the money spent will be made not in Washington, but right at home. And it will be the resident's money not the taxpayer from New Jersey or Oregon.

Can towns make money in the venture capital business? Presently most town officials are like the politicians in Washington, they know how to spend money but don't know how to make it. Under Synergistic Capitalism, public officials will have to be businessmen or businesswomen; they must understand the profit system.

But can towns make money? We need only to look at the success of Mondragon in Spain. Mondragon is not affiliated with any town though it gives a percentage of its profits to adjoining towns to use at the town's discretion. (I believe our towns will be even more successful than Mondragon.) Mondragon was phenomenally successful though it had no help from the Franco government in Madrid because Mondragon is located in the Basque sector of Spain which has wanted its independence from Spain. And Mondragon fought for the royalists during the Spanish Civil War of 1936-39 which lost. Nevertheless Mondragon prospered by starting its own bank, attracting the small savings of people of the area by offering a 1% higher rate of interest. With this money it financed Mondragon entrepreneuring.

Why doesn't Synergistic Capitalism encourage entrepreneurs to contact Venture Capital firms instead of competing with them? Venture Capital firms are interested in making huge profits. Very few business plans are backed. Maybe one in a thousand plans are accepted. Among these, only one in eighty are highly profitable. Unlike Venture Capitalists, Synergistic Capitalism will not cull through the applicants to find the one that will make a killing. Synergistic Capitalism with its voluntary help (everyone in the town must donate weekly service to the community), low overhead, and a research system, will HELP people make a profit. If a great profit, great; if a small profit, that's great too. (If a corporation makes one dollar profit, that's fine because the corporation has provided jobs for many residents thus being quite profitable for the town and its residents.)

What about a salary cap? Won't that eliminate the talented MBA's who can manage successfully? This is the old argument about elitism, that only those in the upper class have the talent and creativity. There's even a group that insists that Shakespeare couldn't have written his plays and sonnets because he didn't have the education or family background. Nonsense.

True, lots of men have made money by cheating and taking advantage of others which "common people" maybe wouldn't have done. [Boot believes that many people in the higher echelon of government and business have low consciousnesses (LQ's)]. And, true, those without money often have a blockage in their subconscious to making money; but blockages can be eliminated and most of us can contribute to make America more prosperous if given a bit of encouragement.

Talent abounds. And Mondragon had no problem finding managers with their low pay scale and management turnover was very low.

Talent too can be attracted with long range stock options which are worthless unless profits are increased. But our town will not offer any "golden parachutes."

So would Synergistic Capitalism encourage entrepreneurs? If you were Lee Iacocca, would you work for a salary seven time that of your lowest employee? Maybe not. Instead you would probably start your own company thus increasing prosperity. Multiply this by thousands of executives who make astronomical wages and you could have a prosperous America for all, not just the one percent...

NOTE: The information about Mondragon is from a report presented in TAB A which was written years ago. Whether Mondragon has continued its original beliefs is unknown. But the principles upon which it gained success are known and presented in this proposal.

CONCLUSION:

A solution to revitalizing our economy is Synergistic Capitalism. It combines the resources of a town with the talents, creativity, energies, and enthusiasm of the individual to encourage capitalism. We presently are not tapping the talents of the individual. Big government, big business, big cities seem oblivious of this treasure. The City States of ancient Greece and Renaissance Italy somehow did tap this greatest of Nature's miracles. Today we still reap the wealth these individuals produced. And today we can design an economic system where people can develop their potential and not depend on the dole. A new Renaissance in business, in the arts, in learning, and in living can result.

The object is not to create anything but billionaires. Instead Synergistic Capitalism's aim is to encourage profitable businesses, creativity, industry and a sense of community. Pride in ones own worth, appreciation of his fellowman, prosperity for the town, and civic pride can result.

Fun is also important. Is there any reason why work can't be a joyous experience? Synergistic Capitalism can introduce the joy of developing an idea; perfecting and marketing this idea; and reaping the rewards. Entrepreneuring could maybe replace baseball as our national sport.

By adopting Synergistic Capitalism maybe man will again enter a new era that the gifted and gentle Alfred North Whitehead predicted. "If there is to be a new Renaissance in the Western World," he said, "it will take place in the American Middle West." Colorado is almost smack dab in the center of our country.

EPILOGUE

As you have probably noticed, this approach assumes we will start with a brand new town in a virgin setting. But what about the cities and towns already built? (Incidentally when someone asked Frank Lloyd Wright what to do about Chicago, he replied, "Tear it down [and start over.]"

Maybe a coop similar to Mondragon could be started. It would be voluntary with those joining paying a membership fee (like becoming a member of a golf club-country club) and contributing their expertise and labor while benefiting from the profit.

Or maybe an area of a city could be torn down and a "Light City" built. (Won't the new city be a light to help awaken mankind? Won't those who join be enlightened?)

Personally I believe Light Cities and Synergistic Capitalism will become so successful they will be exported to undeveloped and developed nations around the world. They will help usher in, I believe, the new Age of Aquarius and aid in the "Shift of the Ages...

NOTES

NOTES

NOTES

NOTES

NOTES